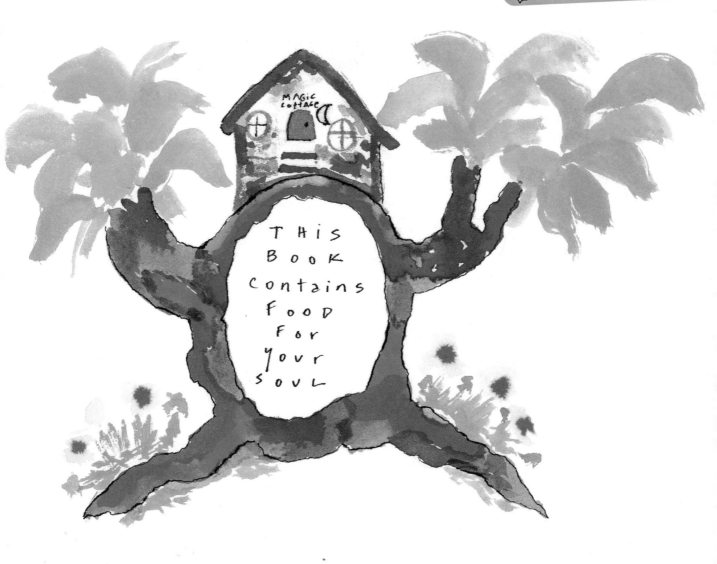

HOW TO BE AN ARTIST

STAY loose. learn to WATCH snails.
plant impossible GARDENS. invite
someone Dangerous to teA. MAKE
little signs that SAY Yes! and post
them All over Your HOUSE. MAKE Friends
with Freedom & uncertainty. look FORWARD
TO DREAMS. CRY DURING MOVIES. SWING
AS HiGH AS YOU can On A swingset,
BY MOONLIGHT. CULTIVATE MOODS. refuse
TO "Be responsible." DO iT FOR love.
TAKE loTs OF naps. Give Money AWAY.
DO iT NOW. THE Money will Follow.
Believe in MAGiC. lAUGH A loT.
CeleBrATe every GORGeous MOMent.
TAKE MOONBATHS. HAVe WiLD
iMAGiNiNGs, TransForMATiVe DReAMS,
AND perfecT CALM. DRAW On the WALLS.
reAD eVeryDAY. iMAGine YOURSeLF
MAGiC. GiGGle with CHiLDren. listen
TO OLD people. Open up. Dive in. Be Free.
Bless YourseLF. Drive AWAY FeAR.
PLAY with everything. entertain
Your inner CHiLD. YOu Are innocent.
BuilD A FORT with Blankets. GeT WeT.
HuG Trees.
write love letters.

Inspiration Sandwich

stories to inspire our creative freedom

BY SARK

Celestial Arts
Berkeley California

"Autobiography in five short chapters"
By Portia Nelson from The Courage to Heal
by Laura Davis & Ellen Bass © 1988

Yes

Jupiter

ISBN:
0-89087-
678-9

SARK
Hand
printed
THIS
BOOK
For You
and
painted
Front
and
BACK
covers

BOOK
Production
By the
Glowing
Mary ann
anderson

LIBRARY OF CONGRESS
CATALOGING-in-PUBLICATION DATA
SARK / inspiration sandwich:
stories to inspire our creative
freedom
1. Conduct of Life
2. Creative Ability - CHALLenges,
   exercises, etc.
3. SELF Actualization - exercises,
   CHALLenges, etc.
I Title
BF637.C55 S28 1992
158 -- dc20

92-20715
CIP

Printed in our United States of America

0 9 8 7 6 5 4 3 2 1
95 94 93 92
First Printing, 1992

This book is food for your soul, and a bubble bath for your spirit! It is a guide to keeping your creativity alive, and I wrote it for you.

In the SARK tradition, it was written while lying down, in PAJAMAS, and in between naps.

My first job was at age 4 as the wake up fairy in Kindergarten. I had a magic wand, and touched each sleeping child. I still have that magic wand.

I believe in waking up creative spirits.

v

We are each inspired treasures, with creative gifts to share.

The world needs your gifts!

This book is meant to be nibbled and tasted in no particular order.
  If you can manage to be in pajamas while reading it, that would be wonder-full, and lying in bed with pajamas on is even better!

But, if you happen to be in the clothed, vertical world, at least take your shoes off.

Try this:
Pick a number between

one and forty-six

Then, turn to the following table of contents and see what chapter you've chosen.

THERE ARE MIRACLES ALL
AROUND US

MIRACLE:
an incandescent,
AMAZING event or
MOMENT, BIG or SMALL

THE MIRACLE is YOU

TABLE of Contents

invite someone Dangerous to teA

cv.

While Housesitting A Mansion on Russian Hill in San Francisco, My neighbors told me I reminded them of A woman in the neighborhood.

"She's in Her late eighties, and HAS ARt studios in Her House and seems Quite wiLD."

I cAlled Her, and introduced Myself, and she said,

"Oh why yes, DeAr, why Don't you come to teA on Thursday?"

That FABulous woman and I HAD teA every weeK For 5 years, and it wAs Quite Dangerous, inDeed.

1

THe Danger of entrancing conversation, Daring emotional exchanges, and impossibly Delicious chocolate cake. We formed a strong Bond over tea, over the years.

earl grey with cream

After Her Death, I Began Hosting tea parties at the St. Francis Hotel for other Dangerous women.
We wear hats, and Gloves, and tell outrageous stories...

see you at the Saint Francis!

Miriam's Chair ♡

2

HUG Trees

Trees love Being HUGGED. The secret to HUGGinG trees is to close your eyes so you won't Feel Shy. IF you HUG A tree long enoUGH, it will HUG you BACK.

*Being HUGGED BACK Feels WARM and BARKy. You MiGHt Grin.

FOLLOW A CHILD

A CHILD'S WORLD IS MADE OF SPIRIT AND MIRACLES. WE SOMETIMES THINK THAT CHILDREN SHOULD FOLLOW US, LISTEN TO US, BECOME LIKE US.

FOLLOW A CHILD CLOSELY FOR AN HOUR. NOT TO TEACH OR TO DISCIPLINE, BUT TO LEARN, AND TO LAUGH.

MY FRIEND EDIE AND I WERE TALKING ON THE PHONE, WHEN HER TWO CHILDREN MEREDITH AND CLAIBORNE, INTERRUPTED US WITH THEIR SHRIEKS AND GIGGLES. EDIE SAID;

"OH MY GOD. THEY'RE STOMPING ON RITZ CRACKERS IN THEIR BARE FEET. REMEMBER HOW GOOD THAT FELT? I CAN'T WATCH.

I Don't want to stop them,
But I can't WATCH."

SHe went into another room,
and we continued our conversation..
Her willingness to Allow Ritz
cracker stomping led me to write:
"How to really love A CHILD."

My eight year OLD Friend, stephanie
comes over to Draw on my WAlls and read
my newest writings.

THis particular Day, I Felt angry
AT A Friend, and Decided to Ask
Stephanie's ADvice.

"WHAT Do you Do when you're really
MAD AT A Friend?" I AskeD.

She thought for a moment.

"Oh, that! Well. Usually you wait until one person forgets, and then that one calls up the other one and says 'Do you want to play?'"

How to be friends again wait until one person forgets

Celebrate an old person

or:

We called my grandfather "Boppa." When I was ten, he had a playhouse built for me and installed in our backyard. It had sliding glass windows, a tile floor, dutch doors and electricity! I was in ten year old heaven.

I declared myself to be a writer and immediately "moved in" to my little house.

Then I decided I wanted a horse and asked Boppa. He said;

"O.K. let's see about it."

He went and got a yellow legal pad and sat with me at the dining room

TABle. We BeGan listinG All the tAsKs
anD expenses AssociAteD with owninG
A Horse: BrusHinG, FeePinG, exercisinG.
etc. Before lonG, the PAGe WAs completely
FVll, anD I looKeD up anD SAiD;

"BoppA, I Don't Think
I want A Horse After All."

He looKeD surpriseD, anD
put the pAD AWAy.

There Are certain OLD people
WHo can HeLp you Grow into yourseLF
Better. He WAs one.

Care of A Horse
1. FeePinG
2. BrusHinG
3. exercisinG
4. SAPPle, BriDle
   HArness
5. SHoe repair
6. STAБles
7. HAy ; ALFALFA
8. VeT Bills
9. CAre ; Attention
10. unexpecteD expes.

Swing as high as you can, on a swingset, by moonlight cir.

Swinging soothes nerves.
Swinging by moonlight is sacred.
Swing until your arms grow tired and your feet are ready to touch the earth again.

All your swinging memories will return. Remember the feeling of loving hands in the small of your back, pushing? Remember being afraid you would swing up and over the top? Remember letting go, and leaping off the swing, safely onto grass or sand?

Go ahead. Swing back into childhood...

9

WEAR PAJAMAS to A Drive in MOVIe

cn

Just Before sunset, you were Bundled into your PAJAMAS and into the car, to A Drive in MOVie. PerHAPS you laid on the car's WARM HOOD with an OLD BlankeT or sleeping BAG, All snuGGly in your PAJAMAS, on A WARM summer night.

WeAr PAJAMAS More often! one time, I BoarDed A plane in A Flannel nightGown and Hiking Boots. People Do stare, But only CHILDren Ask Questions. "MOMMY, why is THAT lady in Her nightGown?"

In chicAGo, My frienD anD I HAD
to cHange planes, anD I WALKeD
through the Airport in thAT FlanneL
niGHTGown.
A MaN PASSeD US, JinGLinG the cHanGe
in His pockeT anD SMiLinG.
"Nice PAJAMAS!" He SAiD.
My FrienD responDeD,
"Hi, BoB!" I wonDereD How sHe
Knew HiM, anD AskeD Her.
"DiDn't you recoGnize HiM? THAT
WAS BoB Hope
   anything can HAPPen in PAJAMAS.

11

DEVELOP an ASTOUNDING APPETITE FOR BOOKS

BOOK recipes

I like to savor and digest a hearty selection of books: the smell of paper is an appetizer. A deep biography is good with a pinch of short stories, and a sauce of romance novel mixed generously with an assortment of essays, travel stories and memoirs. Simmer until sauce thickens, and then add one strong self help book. Take a nap. Arise to stir up the mixture and begin again. Entire affair can be baked in 3-4 hours at a very high temperature and should feed one person until pleasantly stuffed. Calories: 0. Fat: none. Carbohydrates: 0. P.S. Fiction and poetry can be scattered throughout and will vary flavor tremendously.

learn to watch snails
cir

Snails are tiny prophets in our gardens. Moving slowly, carrying their own homes, snails are kind to other snails.

There is a snail in my garden I call the "city snail." Its shell had been crushed or cracked, and it had built a new shell with part of

a match book that said: Win $10,000! Snail watching is best by moonlight, when it is very late and quiet.

13

Wrap yourself in A thick Blanket, and
sit Down near some snails.
  IF you're lucky, you might see them
making love. One time, I laid on my
stomach watching 2 snails make love
for hours. It looked so slippery and erotic,
I felt shy! Later, I found out that
snails have both sets of sex organs!

IF snails ever Bother your plants, you
can ask them to stop. Snails are
Quite responsive to kind requests.
OR, if you have stubborn snails,
make a compost pile
Just for them.

14

CATS Are angels with FUR

Surrender, You Are now entering the tunnel of CAT love. it's soft, it's WARM, it's CAT·A·Tonic. Some little known CAT secrets: CATS Are POLKA Dotted under their FUR. CATS love lemonade on A HOT DAY. CATS refuse to play scrabble. CATS will pay your rent if you let them. CATS HAVE not nine lives, but two: theirs, then yours. Some CATS MAKE pay offs to FLEA gangs. C.A.T. stands for Clever Anatomical Tricks. CATS know How to cozy up. CATS sleep circular. CATS invented naps. Kiss your CAT. A FUR BALL is not A toy. ADOPT A CAT... it will take over your Life (and you wont mind)

DEDICATED to: _____
(CAT name or names Here)

(Dedicated to Jupiter the Yes cat)

Kitty love
CAT naps
WILD CAT
CAT BUDDIes

DOGS Are Miracles with PAWS

A DOG's nose in the PALM of your Hand can cure ALMOST anything. Dogs Are MADE of love and Fur. Let your DOG TAKE you FOR A WALK. DOGS Are A sure thing. Some little KNOWN DOG secrets: DOGS HAVE no secrets. Dogs Are like vanilla ice cream: reliABly Delicious. DOGS Are wise AGents Directly FROM Heaven. if you HAD A tail, wouLDn't you WAG it? There Are no BAD DOGS. Be your DOG's Best FRienD. DOGS Like Dancing, Drive-in Movies anD Dreaming. GOD MADE DOGS anD spelled His own name BACKwARDS! DOGS MAKE GReAT THERAPISTS. Kiss your DOG All the time. Some DOGs Are nAP DOGS. DOGs inventeD unconDitional LOVE. DOGS Are PARTY AnimaLs. Apply DOG loGic to Life: eAt well, Be loveD, Get petteD, sleeP A lot, DReam OF A leAsH-Free WORLD.

Live your DOG's Life!

(PAws For a Miracle!)

DEDICATED to PunKy, my First Dog love

DEDICATED to: _____
DOG name or names Here

TAKE lots oF NAPS

I AM KNOWN AS the
"NAP QVEEN." WHEN I
WAS in elementary school,
I WOULD Come Home For
lunch, and For 42 minutes,
change into My PAJAMAS
and take A miniature NAP.

NAPs Are necessary to My
creative LiFe.

A GOOD NAP can Be HarD to FIND.
SNEAK AWAY, and set yourself up
For the perfect NAP.

A SMAll SNACK, your FAVorite pillow,
and A certain KinD OF QuieT.

CLOUD cover

Perhaps something to read, and if you can manage, a shaft of sunlight.

All at once, you sail away into a nap, where tangled nerves are untied, and where time stops.

Guilt and expectations are not welcome in napland. You can always find a reason. Find more reasons to let naps take you!

let the book fall shut

naps forever

napland

18

write A simple loving letter

THank you

WRITE MORE love letters ⑤

Letters Are cHances For the souL to speAk. A Mood cAptured in the FiBers oF the pAper, A worLD in an envelope wHicH will not exist untiL it is openeD.

Love letters MAke love stAy VisiBle. You can ruB it, sMell it, toucH it, sHAre it, anD sleep with it unDer your pillow.

yes

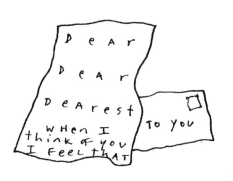

DEAr
DEAr
DEArest
WHen I
think of you
I Feel tHAT

TO YOU

Write A love letter on A BED sHeet
  with MAGic MARkers sleep unDer it.
Write A love letter on the SiDeWALK
  with purple CHALK reAlly BiG.
Write A love letter in the sanD anD leAve
it to WASH AWAY .
Write A love letter to yourseLF, listing All
of your finest QuaLities. RAve ABout you.
  Then, MAiL it to your House.
Write A love letter on A cotton SCARF with
InDiA ink. Give it to someone .
DesiGn your own stationery anD use it.
MAKe A love letter BOX anD keep romAnce in it.
20

TAKE MOONBATHS

Cr.

WALKING AT MIDNIGHT is very GOOD For MoonBAThing. I CArry A WALKing stick And Become invisible to any trolls.

one nocturnAL WALK, I SAW A SMALL Sign THAt SAID "MAGic cottAGe For A very SPeciAL Person, secludeD GArDen with Fern trees."

I FounD A coBBleD lane, and A MiniAture Gate with A stick HOLDing the GAte SHut. I PeereD inside to see A secret GArDen, And A tiny cottAGe neArLy HiDDen BY PALM FronDs. I knew it WAS My Home.

incidentally, I
didn't have money, but
I couldn't let that
stop me from having
a magic cottage!
I sold artwork, asked
for favors and received
help from family and
friends.
Children often ask;
"why is the magic
cottage magic?"
I suppose it is because I believe
in magic!

Allow yourseLf
to FeeL ricH
without money

Many people wHo HAVe
lots oF Money never FeeL
riCH.
Feeling ricH is Born oF simple things:
GooD HeALth, comFort, FreeDom anD
lAVGhter AlonG with BeinG well loveD.
Money is important, BVt inciDentAL.
reMeMBer this AFFiRMAtion: Yov
Are welcome everywHere.
   I've Been visiting PArADise IslanD
in the BAHAMAS For Zo yeArs.

I USED to Go there without A Dime.

One time, I slept on A CHAise lounge CHAir By the pool For 2 weeks! I GAVE MY BAGGAGE to the concierge and CHAnged into MY evening clothes in the BAthrooM.

WHen I Moved to San Francisco FroM HAWAii, I HAD $35, So I FounD A BoArDinG House thAt CHArGeD $30 For the week.

Then, I FounD A FAMous and eleGant San Francisco Hotel loBBy to sit in and DrAW.

I MADE A SMALL sign THAT reAD:
"ARtist AVAilABle for Dinner" AND SAT on
A WONDErFUL CHAiR in the loBBy of the
Saint Francis Hotel with My SKETCHBOOK.
     Four sweet GVys From new yorK
SHOWED Up AND invited Me to Dinner.

They HAD A CorporAte
Suite At the HoteL THAT
woULD Be eMpty the NexT
DAY, AND AskeD iF I
wANTED to occupy it!
(I DiD).

     Learn to step liGHTly
From one MirAcle to the NexT.
Feeling riCH is AVAilABle to anyone,
At any time. especially to you!

25

eAT MaNGoeS NAKeD

I Always lAuGH WHeN People wHo
DoNT kNow me well, thiNk Im So
"Free." close FrieNDs will tell you
tHAT I HAVe MaNy FeArs aND iDiosyn
crAcies.
JuST tAke MaNGoes. I Do Not eAT theM
NAKeD. It souNDs GooD, But I cAnT
BeAr the thouGHT oF eNDuriNG tHAT
kiND oF stickiNess. one time, A FrieND
iN the BAHAMAS kNew I WAS coming
aND FloAteD A lot oF MaNGoes iN
My swimmiNG POOL. THAT WAS the

only time I've ever eaten them naked!

People frequently ask me about being creatively alive and how to get "unstuck." For myself, getting unstuck is a daily, sometimes hourly, process. I think it is about little things. Altering your routine as much as possible:

Buy purple flowers and put them on a hat.

rake leaves and quit in the middle.

Don't check your mail for 3 days.
read the newspaper in the opposite order.
Break a dish you never liked.
Wear hideously colored socks.
If you're in a hurry, do things slowly.
These "little things" will lead you into a new mood.
A new mood will lead you into new creativity.
Then immediately take a nap and let it all soak in.

EAT inspiring FOODS

let the WORLD HEAL YOU

BUY A TOY FOR YOURSELF

lie DOWN A lot

let MIRACLES FIND YOU

PUT FOOD coloring in your BATHWATER

ADMIRE YOUR SELF

Open A BOOK to any PAGE, let WHAT your eye sees, CHANGE YOU

BE A DREAMER

LAUGH YOUR HEAD OFF (then, GET it BACK!)

BuiLD Forts with Blankets

REMEMBER the SAFety oF A GooD Fort?
BEDSPREADS DRAPED AcRoss cHAirs,
WEiGHTED DowN By Giant BooKS, with
A tunneL leaDinG under the CARD tAble.
    MAyBe there WAS A Hole in one oF
the BEDSPREADS, put there So you
CouLD Peer out, unseen.

YOU MIGHT DRAG A STACK OF COMIC BOOKS
and A row of cookies into your Fort, and
Stay there All DAY in the DUll Glow of
BEDSPREAD LiGHT.

The Fort WAS your
refuge, your secret
SPoT, the interior
untouched BY
ADULT HanDS or
eyes.

It WAS A WORLD
you Built For
yourself.

PerHAPS iF
your Best FrienD CAME over, you
MiGHT MAKe endless PlAYinG CARD

Houses inside the Fort, or eat so many Cheez Doodles that your face turned orange.

Now as an adult, I build Forts with my cat Jupiter. We let the Down Comforters hang down all around the loft bed, and stay in there playing silly games.

Sometimes, we sing songs and snap rubber bands, and dream of a world filled with Forts made of blankets...

Dry Your clothes in the sun

There is A rare smell that gets into clothes dried in the sun. It is A scent of waves and porches and summer grass. It is A fresh, luxurious, simple aroma that brings A smile and A hugging of the sheets.

There is A long wooden stairway that leads to my rooftop clothesline. The wind is always flag snapping off the bay, and I can look down

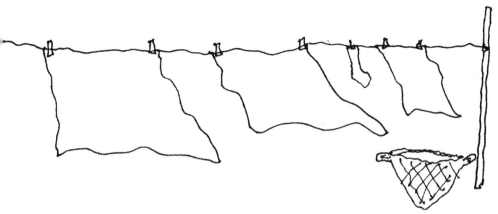

On the treetops. one time, I
stood up there for awhile trying
to figure out:
When exactly does that good smell
Get into the clothes?
Like many good things, it is
Mysterious and untraceable.

Drink sunsets

There is a tiny park in San Francisco that is perfect for watching the sun set. It's a bird's nest of a park up a long flight of steps made out of railroad ties. There are red tile rooftops and an assortment of brightly colored hummingbirds. I stand in honor of the sun retreating. I watch keenly as the light changes,

and windows glow golden across the
Bay.
There is a certain purple sky in
San Francisco that appears at
twilight. It is a color and shape
I never see anywhere else. I like
to observe the close of the day with
the sun's setting.

especially in a city, I think we
dearly miss nature if we don't
make a point to be there and absorb
Her blessings.

How to take a miracle WALK

Bring a small BAG PACKED for extraterrestrial travel. Wear a brightly colored HAT and pick a Destination that Delights you.

Along the WAY, communicate with every animal and child you see. notice colors. DreAM while moving. If it's raining, this counts as a Double miracle WALK.

Wear an outlandish rain HAT and stomp in every puddle you see.

Be open to the miracles. This means;
Follow your in·sight. Climb a tree,
peer over a fence, sit on a park
bench and wait ~ miracles are
some times shy.
Bring a notebook or sketch pad and
position yourself in some extraordinary
spot. Let yourself be guided on paths
leading to miracles.
Let yourself "pleasure walk." No errands,
or time restraints. No plans!
anything could happen, and probably
will.
Here are the results of 3 of my "miracle
walks."

Greenwich steps 2:30 PM

I met her, as she crouched in a garden of baby tears, which is appropriate, since her mother was Grace Marchant, founder of the Marchant Gardens on the Filbert steps.

When I asked for her best gardening advice, she replied briskly, "Water, water and water some more! Rely on the earth to tell you what she wants, not some book!"

Valetta spoke of moving to Telegraph Hill "way back when" and paying $30 a month in rent.

"We didn't have much money for food, but we just had to have that cottage on the hill! Friends would bring sacks of potatoes when they came to visit us.

Now, of course, we own our cottage and these buildings around it.

I would tell anyone just starting out to, "Hold fast to your dream!"

3:20 pM PALACE OF FINE ARTS

Swans MATE for Life, WHICH Always MAKES Me HAPPY to Think ABout.
   THese swans encircle the PandorA Art piece – an opening in
the wAter with stAirs leading Down.
   I want to Fling Myself into the pond and take Those steps into
another world. A wAtery reALM, A FISH PArADise, stAirwAy to
Neptunian Heaven. The swans in A singular Duet, their long
necks carving still pond waters. The light on the pond is A
Certain luminous Green... many spirits HAVE SAT Here...

41

Powell & Geary 5:20pm

He calls himself Agape, which means "love without ego" and he has been homeless by choice for fifteen years. He studies Lao Tzu, and plays the flute, and was once a professional photographer. He says "I got tired of "human doings" instead of human beings."

I asked if he ever gets uncomfortable being outside, and he snorted and waved his arm at the passing crowd on Powell street. "Them! They're uncomfortable being outside! Do you think they're examining any truths?"

extend surprising invitations

My friend Christina said to me, "want to come over and eat Poptarts and watch movies?" I rapidly did an "Adult" calculation: Poptarts = a headache, movies = time spent doing "nothing."

Then, I let my "inside child" take over. Her house was set up as a movie cave. Futons, cushions and pillows covered the floor, and it was dark, cool and quiet. Boxes of poptarts were stacked by the toaster. We bundled in and did nothing but eat poptarts and watch movies, and I loved every second! No headache! We need to extend surprising invitations and accept them.

We told our friend Deidre to be Available for A surprise on Her 20th Birthday. Then, we picked A Beach with an easy 3 mile trail leading to it, and Hiked in With A Table, White tablecloth, A vase of Spring flowers, candles, silver trays of Food, A Birthday carrot cake, A bottle of Champagne, A white waiters Jacket (and A "Waiter" to wear it) and A large Black umbrella. We set up this scene not far from the edge of the ocean, and not long before the sun's setting.

JoAnn told me she wanted to give me a "Magic" tour of Berkeley. I got into her car, and found a white envelope with my name typed on it. I opened it to read:

"SARK's Magic tour of Berkeley"
A wonderous list followed of enchanted places to visit.

After several hours, I was lying on my back in a magnificent rose garden saying,

"Please! I can't absorb any more Magic!"

SARK's
Magic
itinerary
of
Berkeley

"Hansel i, Gretel
2. The society of Jesus
Go Co-op
and the secret waterfall
3. On the trail of
Isadora Duncan
and the temple
of the wind
4. an abundance
of roses

45

Friendships thrive on surprises. Make a gingerbread figure of your friend.
Send a letter to your friend with one Ballet ticket inside...
Meet her there.
Give your friend a bag of fortune cookies — only you write all the fortunes!
   One of my best friends was named Miriam, and at the time she was 89 years old. I came to visit her, and she opened her front door to greet me wearing a gorgeous teal blue silk suit.

I COMPLIMENTED Her and SHE SAID
"Thank you" LAUGHING, and Gently
stepped out of the SKiRt and took OFF
the JACKeT.
STANDING there in Her slip, SHe SAiD,
"Here! I think it WOULD look GReAT
on you."

The FABULOUS teAL Blue suit

A MAZE YOURSELF

WE ALL DO things THAT ARE AMAZING.

I roDE A Bicycle 3,000 Miles aND FELT AMAZED the whole WAY.

My Brother aNDrew TALKED Me into CLIMBING HALF DOME in Yosemite~ the BACK WAY BY trAIL~ There is A CABLE STAIRWAY pouNDED into the rocks aND Very steep. I FroZe HALFWAY UP in A paNic ATTACK aND AMAZED MYseLF By continuING to the top!

48

When it was time to write my first book, I heard so many voices in my head that said, No! I amazed these voices by shouting Yes! and writing my book. Invite your fears in, then tell them to sit down and shut up!

When I first began getting massages, I felt very sensitive to pain, and asked for very light massages. Now, I am amazed to be having deep tissue bodywork and learning that conscious breathing can make pain go away.
I continue to amaze myself!

SHARE yourself on the telephone

SHE LIVED iN.A PHoNe Booth

THis DRAWING is oF Me. I live anD lAVGH on the Phone. Here Are soMe of My "telephonic svGGestions:" HAVe Fun on the PHone! IF you're HAVinG Fun, the other person will Also, anD ABsolute MiRacles can tAKe place.

Secrets to HAVinG Fun on The PHone: relax. BReAthe. lAVGH. Let your personALity out to play. IF you're vsvAlly sHy, pRactice BeinG BRAVe on the PHone. IF yov GeT sCAReD, yov can Always JvsT sAy GooDBye!

empathize with the other person: If
you're calling a car rental agency,
spend a few extra moments cheering
up and complimenting the rental agent.
   Imagine how you might feel being
at that job, and what you would like
to hear.

   Say something
slightly outrageous:
   We all want to
be delighted or
surprised.
   When I call for
an airline ticket,
I might ask if

Just remember:
every time you
talk on the phone,
it forms a cartoon
bubble that floats
around for a long
time.

THere's A special FAre for people wearing raincoats or standing on their HEAD AT the Airport. Then, the ticket AGent and I can LAUGH together and Become partners in Finding The Best ticket price. (I Always Fly AT A GREAT Discount.)

Help people to Become involved: IF you can SHAre something oF yourseLF, people Are MucH More inspired to HeLp. Recently, I Hired A tax consultant,

I JUST LOVE

You and Me on the PHone

and we agreed to work together by mail and phone. When I sent in my list of expenses and deductions, I enclosed a catalog of my work, with a photograph of me and a friendly note.

She loved the visual involvement, and now calls my answering machine with laughing messages, and our talks on the phone are easy and fun (yes, about taxes!)

Also, after doing my taxes, she sent me her bill, with a discount for my laughter, my answering machine messages, and my personality!

Have more fun with answering machines!

My phone is your phone... (except for long distance)

STAMP out Conformity! Leave no normal messages. We all know about leaving a message after the beep. Be experimental.

Remember to enjoy yourself while leaving someone a message. They'll hear the laughter in your voice and love to hear your words.

I like to think of my voicemail as "answering machine theatre:" A tiny electronic stage. I invent characters to "take the stage" and put on performances.

Currently, my message is just a recording of me laughing. It causes people to laugh in return, and we need it! Telephones are one electronic miracle after another.

answering machine theatre

54

Celebrate every Gorgeous Moment

I Believe that I have Developed A special sight for Gorgeous Moments. They occur Around us All the time, in the most ordinary settings, But you Must Pay Attention.

There is A Bus Driver I call "Popsicles and Broccoli" Because He told Me that He eats A lot of Both to stay in shape. Mostly, He celebrates every Person Getting on the Bus with an incandescent smile and words to Help people Laugh.

everyone HAS someThing GorGeous to
offer if we TAKe the time to listen.
  One time, while
riding A cABle cAr,
I HeArD A man say,
"I WAS the cookie cAptain!"
I knew immediately WHAT
He WAS TAlKing ABout, and
cAlleD out;
"I WAS the WAKe up fairy!"
Soon, The whole cABle cAr full of people
were cAlling out the "JoBs" they HAD
in KinDerGArten!
I f we remember THAT eAch of us
HAS A smAll cHilD insiDe, we can

Feel free to reach in and be truly
friendly.
Miracles happen between people all the
time, pressed into those tiny moments
that might go unseen without
"Miracle moment collectors"
Try walking around with an emotional
net to capture
miracles in.
Then, share them
with others.
We all need more
miracles!
Learn to be a radiant
human, and then shine
on others.

I like to WALK, and Be Guided By my
Feelings About where to go.
   On this DAY, I went into A BARBerSHOP
   Because the BARBer WAS exuBerantly playing
                        A clArinet.
                           He WAS Greek,
                           and Full OF Joy.
                           I SHAreD SOMe
                           Money worries
                           with HiM, and
                           He SAiD,

                           "ID rAther
                           spenD one DAY
                           in totAL FreeDom,
                           than 50 yeArs
                           in PARtiAL cAptivity."
           I leFt The BARBersHOP
           very ricH.

Rich in my purpose and guided by my dream, floating on that "Gorgeous Moment."

I frequently ask God for "signs."

one evening, I was sitting in a small cafe, eating Madeleine cookies for the first time.

I felt sad and confused about some issues and prayed for guidance.

I felt drawn suddenly to go into a bookstore and take a book from the shelf,

I opened the book to just this sentence:

"WHoever eATS MADeleine's will Be surely and certainly UPLIFteD in All ways."

So Here We Are, in our rare and Precious Lives, surrounded BY Gorgeous Moments Begging to Be noticed and celeBrAteD.

Go! CeleBrate!

3PM
GOLDEN GATE PARK
CAROUSEL

REMEMBER BEING
OLD ENOUGH TO
RIDE ALONE AND
BACKWARDS?

61

MAKE FrienDS with FreeDOM & uncertainty

One oF My FAvorite Heroes oF this type oF Living is nameD RoBert. His LiFe is CONDENSED into A FeW Boxes, anD the rest is Deep, ABunDant trAvel.

He Might return WEArinG A cloAK Woven in TunisiA, anD the next time you see HiM, He HAS Given it AWAY anD FOunD another COAT on A street corner.

His trAveL MoMents Are SHAreD in His Writings, PHotoGrAPHs anD FiLMS. I BASK in His Glow OF FreeDOM anD uncertainty.

He is constantly recreAtinG His LiFe, anD I Get nourisHMent FroM WATCHinG.

the
edge

I believe that during my years of living "on the edge," I did learn to make friends with freedom and uncertainty, and that now I can reclaim that friendship whenever I begin a new book, or create something that has never been, before.

My very dear and delightfull friend Larry was an attorney, and asked me to make a poster for him called "How to be a Happy Lawyer." So, I created one as a gift for him, and as I sat there with my work, this is what materialized.

How to Be A HAPPY LAwyer

Quit

WHen you open the tiny Door, it sAys, "Quit"

Cri

I AM not AGainst lawyers, it just seemed to Me thAt the rest oF the World WAs cAlling LARry. So He DiD Quit, For A GranD reAson: A Full FellowSHip AT VC Berkeley, For A MAster's Degree in Public policy. LArry HAs A Brilliant MinD anD A very ARtistic, HuMAnistic nature.
He is HAppy anD thriving in His new Life.

Cri

64

My FABUloUS anD very true FrienD Helen tells
Her story: "I WAS WAitressinG anD GettinG
My B.A. in WOMen's stUDies. THe WAitress
WorK WASn't FUlFillinG My purpose anyMore,
anD My BODy BeGan eXHiBitinG UnHAPPy
symptoMs. So, the [leAP OF FAith] WAS to
Know ID DO something WONDerFUL, even
iF I DiDn't yet Know WHAt. I tooK My
WAitress sHoes, APron anD leAther orDer
PAD ∼ the "tools" I neeDeD to MAKe Money,
anD turneD them in to the GooDwill."
Helen's leAP oF FAith leD Her to A MAster's
DeGree, anD BeinG The eXecUtive Director
oF The San Francisco chapter oF The national
OrGanizAtion For WoMen, anD now, to
WritinG, anD MAKinG FiLMs. SHe SAys,
  "SometiMes you JUst HAve to PUt
   everyThinG AsiDe anD HAve FAith." 65

Live Juicy

flowers
to
GASP over

Living Juicy Means:
Rolling Down A Bright Grassy Hill,
Sleeping All Day to stay in A Dream,
Definitely taking your shoes off at the
Beach, Dancing to your
Headphone stereo,
Buying Flowers that
Make you Gasp, Kissing
Puppies, running
Just for Fun, and
Imagining yourself
        M A G i C

I think it's possible to forget How
[ALive] we really Are.
We can Become Dry and tired, Just
existing, instead of really Living.
We need to remind ourselves of the
Juice of Life, and MAKe thAT A
HABit.
Find those plAces inside
ThAT JUMP For JOY, and
Do things thAT Bring OUT
your BesT, MOsT MAGiC
SeLF.
Keep Doing them!

J   U   M   P
      F o r
   J   o   Y

Sometimes, iF I Become De·presseD,

it's usually because I need to express
something.
We all have paintings and music and
writing inside of us.
Keep supplies close
at hand: Brushes, pens,
giant boxes of crayons,
paints and pads of
paper ～ the tools of
expression.
Make a letter writing
box, and keep papers,
stamps, envelopes, pens
and an address book
inside.
Then, put it all aside and run outside
to say goodnight to the sun!

crayons

My letter box
★ ⊙ · · , ♊
STAMP out conformity

One of my teachers of "Living Juicy" was definitely Miriam. She was 87 when she called to invite me to a drawing class at her house.

"We're using a male model ～ but we'll have to draw fast ～ we don't want flaccid muscles!"

After class, we ate chocolate donuts the size of life preservers and sat by the fire, telling stories.

Live Juicy! Your aliveness will make the angels laugh.

Drive away Fear

I AM AFRAID OF VEGETABLES.
AFRAID THAT I'M HURTING
THEM, OR THAT I DON'T KNOW
HOW TO HANDLE THEM, OR
THAT I WON'T LIKE HOW THEY
TASTE. I DO LIKE TO EAT THEM,
ESPECIALLY WHEN SOMEONE
ELSE HAS COOKED OR CHOPPED THEM.
I AM AFRAID OF MORE ORDINARY THINGS TOO:
NEEDLES, BITING DOGS, POISON OAK, VIOLENCE,
BATS, CAR ACCIDENTS... THE LIST GOES ON
FOR A LONG WHILE.
I AM IN THE MIDST OF LEARNING TO FACE

MY FEARS. IT SEEMS THAT FEARS ARE All BASED on these things: illusion and Future thinking, with A side order of "WHAT IF." "WHAT IF THAT truck turns suddenly into our lane" "WHAT IF I'M All Alone AT AGe 80?"
WHAT IF? WHAT IF? WHAT IF?
Yes, FEArs Must Be respected and learned ABout, But they Must not PARAlyze us, or lure us into A HALF-LiFe oF Being AFRAID All the time. I like to think OF My FEArs Being Driven AWAy in A Rolls Royce (For it is true that once you FACE A FEAR, it loses All

of its stuffing, and will sit quietly in the BACK SEAT and DO AS it's told.)

I feel that Fears Drive us away from our true selves innocent Beings. I used to live in DENIAL OF MY FEArs, and to try to cover them up with a "HAPPY FACE."

I now see that my Greatest Growth is Happening with an acceptance of My Fears, of Giving them voices, and learning new ways to DEAL with them.

THank Heavens For therapy, seLF Healing and GOD, Helping me to unravel My FEArs, Because it's A Process I'M AFrAiD to Do Alone!

HAVE WILD iMAGiNINGS,
TRANSFORMATIVE DREAMS AND PERFECT CALM

ONE OF MY FAVORITE GAMES to play in
MY JOURNAL is CALLED: I WANT. I write
"I WANT" AND then let WILD iMAGiNiNGS
MAKE things up. Here is an exAMPLE
FROM MY JOURNAL:
I want to write A BOOK ABOUT MiRACLES.
I want to see A BABY BUFFALo. I
WANT reD rUBBer rainBOots. I want
to EAT BUtterscotCH PUDDiNG AT
MIDNIGHT. I want twin BABY turtles,
A new WALKING stick and clean WHite
SOCKS. I want to CHANGE the

School system in America. I want
to practice on a trapeze, wear new
corduroy pants and have a new
friend who's old.

Transformative dreams await us
each time we sleep. I like to ask
questions before sleeping, and then
dream the answers.

our   pillows   float   us   into   dreams...

Dreams love to guide us and answer questions we're not ready to ask our conscious mind. I do write down all my dreams, and now have hundreds of dreams in my journals to reread for clues to my unconscious.

Dreams are the angels of our spirits.

our spirits will guide us if we listen

75

Perfect CALM seems to come to me in moments.

That first sip of tea.
Watching a spider spin.
First moments of rainfall.
Tucking into bed with clean sheets, just after the light is turned off.

Watch for perfect CALM. I think it loves Attention. I am presently trying to learn more about perfect CALM by meditating. So far, I've meditated once. I've spent a lot of time in extreme moods, and perfect CALM is very new to me. You can think of me, learning to let perfect CALM happen!

plant impossible GArDens

I love it when people SAy, "you can't
Do thAT."
It's like HeAring "I DAre you."
When I went to europe Alone AT AGe 19,
these SAMe people SAiD, "switzerlanD
is very expensive, you can't expect to
Live there."
So oF course, I went to switzerlanD
iMMeDiAtely, anD Met A Man in ZerMAtt,
looking For A Housesitter For His chAlet
thAT HAD JUST Been BuiLt into the siDe
oF A MoUntain, Accessible only By

CHAIRLIFT.

YEARs AGo, in the BAHAMAS, I
HAD no Money, and WAs tired
of sleeping in the lounGe cHAirs
By the pool. I went to one of
the BiG Hotels and AskeD to see
the ManaGer. I TOLD Him THAT I WOULD
like to BABysit or teACH swimming
in exCHanGé For A rooM.
He just lookeD AT Me, anD then reACHeD
into A DrAwer, took out A set of keys
and PusHeD THem ACross the Desk.
"TAke these. I WAS younG AND Broke
once too."

The keys opened the door to a
penthouse on the top floor. I lived there
for a month.
I like to take the impossibles and
make them possible.
I believe that we need to [GO TO]
where we want to be, and the
resources will follow us.
Impossible means I'M possible!
Plant all your impossible gardens,
and see what blooms!

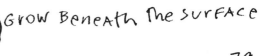

Amazing things grow beneath the surface

Write your own BOOKS!
(Keep A Journal)

AMAZING
stories
of
mine

NoBody else
Can write
WHAT you
write.
NOBODY.

FIND your
own voice!
Then, let
it Be HEARD
All over the
world.

WHen I WAS 26 yeArs OLD,
I HAD to FinD out About
Myself, and Whether or not
I WAS "reAlly" A writer. I'D spent A lot
of time living WilDly, and HAVinG All
Sorts of ADventures, with very little
time for reflection upon those experiences.
    I FounD Myself BACK in Minnesota,
Sitting in the little PlAyHouse thAt
My GranDfather, "BOPPA" HAD BuiLt for Me,
and Where I HAD written My First

BOOK AT AGE 10. I HAD A STACK OF
school composition noteBOOKS, and
I BeGan writing everyDAY.
   My own writing
BoreD Me, But I trieD
to iGnore thAt.
   I reAD everyone's JOURNALS: anais nin,
MAy SArton anD so Many others. I reAD
All of Henry Miller, and every BOOK
Written ABout JOURNAL Keeping.
   THe MessAGe FroM All these writings
WAS cleAr: "Keep writinG."
   So, I DeciDeD to Keep writing
no MAtter WHAT. It worKeD.
   By the eArly 1980's, ID BeGun

To FeeL confineD in My lineD composition
noteBooks, anD BOUGHT A BiG BLACK
BounD JOUrnAL/sketchBook, anD A Box
oF crAyoLA MArkers to Go with it.
By now, I HAD MOVeD to San Francisco
anD WAS living in the Victorian HoteL
OF ARTs anD MUSIC.
My writinG expanDeD in Many WAys
AFter thAt. I wrote in All Different
Colors, Quite lArGe. As L A r G e
AS I Felt like.
It DeliGhteD Me to see those BiG
Color·FUll Books eMerGe.
now, I HAve over 100 oF them.

Since 1989, my journals are smaller in size, and I print quite small, because now that delights me. My journals happen to be written with an eye towards sharing them with others someday. My wonder.full friend Adrienne has begun reading them. So far, she has read 10. I love her immersion in my journal world.

I love journal keeping because it helped me to discover and uncover myself, to en.courage my own bravery, sort out my difficulties with other people, to invent new ways of being, and of seeing, to plan all kinds of adventures and plans, and most of all, to live experiences more than once.

. Twice in the writing, three times in the reading.

I once read that the writer Erica Jong traveled with all her finished and unfinished manuscripts in a suitcase, and showed them to no one. Because then she could be judged.

Having judged myself for years, I can relate to that. I found out that I am indeed, a writer and an artist, and that I have a lot to share with others.

My journals are dear friends, and very creative companions. They are a holder of my dreams, a celebration of moments, a collection of miracles, and a joy to have created.
Write your books. The ones that [only you] can tell.

We all support you!

How to Go out Alone
(and Have a Fabulous time)

People Frequently say to me,
"You went there Alone? I could never do that."

Oh yes, you could!
Pick 3 places that have fascinated you in some way, and let's plan to go there.

Here is the "equipment" I need for a time out with myself.

1. A good book
2. notebook, sketchbook
3. tiny set of paints
4. Change for the phone
5. Feeling safe

I'M Actually A SHy person, so I can offer HELPFUL WAys to set shyness Aside.

I Dress in something that Delights me.

I pretend to be looking For someone.

I Go to the pHone and call a Dear friend, to feel Grounded.

I Definitely talk to strangers.

I set up my "Camp" with A cup of tea, A small snack, A good seat and my sketchbook and watercolors (which I might not actually use.)

I make friends with the service person.

reMinDer: THis is the Best time to
MAKe use oF the AFFirMAtion:
"I AM welcome everyWHere."
I settle in, anD Do some people WATcHinG/
oBserving, MAKinG up stories ABout
some of the people I see.
SoMetimes, I write A note to someone
WHo interests Me, inviting them to
HAve teA.
reMeMBer: A plAce is lucky to HAve
[You] visit it!

I enJoy My own CoMpany, lAUGH AT
MyseLF, anD KnoW thAT MAny ADventures
can HAppen WHen we're willinG to
trAveL Alone.

Then, your 3 places can become familiar
to you, and you can look forward to
"dates" with yourself.
Here is a drawing I did on one of my
"self dates."

1. While I waited for the
Bittersweet chocolate
obsession dessert to arrive,
the bread became an alligator!

2. Then there appeared
an enormous chocolate
pod, complete with
chocolate bowling balls!

in celebration of Deep night

"The Air is filled with the Dreams of the sleeping people."
I am usually awake from midnight until 7 am. It's a rich creative time for me. There aren't any distractions, interruptions, or "things to Do" in the outside world.

There is a certain penetrating kind of quiet at night.

My pen leaps to paper, paints and bits of colored paper are scattered across the floor.

I shuffle around wearing incredibly
wrinkled and well-loved PAJAMAS,
robes, sweatshirts and thick socks.
All sorts of new ideas bloom in the
night. The night time is like special
soil for creative gardens. Usually music accompanies me, and
special kinds of incense, and carefully
chosen lighting. I measure time by
mugs of tea

Being nocturnal is a curious
thing in a world that promotes the
9-5 life. I make no appointments
until after 3pm, and sometimes
people find this odd. (not as odd
as I find 9 am!)

Many times, I AM Blessed to see Both sunrise and sunset. I Find it is imperative to Feel As Free As possible About sleeping. I Cannot "Go to sleep eArly" the night Before, to prepare For some Activity or event The next DAy.

I ClAiM AS MVCH FreeDoM AS possiBle For My sleeping HABits.

I recently reAD ABout some sleep reseArcH thAt WAS Done. The suBject took nAps wHenever He WAS tireD, and DiD As He likeD. He took 10 nAps A DAy, and never neeDeD to sleep More than A Few Hours Altogether. They cAlleD this "MULtiple nApping."

92

I support people taking naps and simply staying in bed whenever the urge is there.

Someday, we will have "nap rooms" in stores, restaurants and airports. Think how grand it will be!

If you have any inclinations to stay up all night, do it. Arrange your life to accommodate your best sleeping style.

Why daylight savings time? Why not night-time spending time?

nap rooms with beds like cool pockets... places to slip into and slide into a dream...

93

Quotes

"DREAMS DON'T
COME TRUE ~
DREAMS ARE TRUE"
RUBY MONTANA

"SO YOU SEE, IMAGINATION
NEEDS MOODLING — LONG,
INEFFICIENT, HAPPY IDLING,
DAWDLING AND PUTTERING."
BRENDA VELAND

"WHY DOES ANYBODY
READ OR WRITE A BOOK?
IF I WANTED TO SEARCH
FOR TRUTH, I COULD FIND
IT IN STORY. STORY CAN
TAKE US FAR, FAR BEYOND
FACT."
MADELEINE L'ENGLE

"BE ALWAYS ECSTATIC.
BE FILLED WITH A
DIVINE INTOXICATION."
HENRY MILLER

"WHOEVER USES THE SPIRIT
THAT IS IN HIM CREATIVELY
IS AN ARTIST. TO MAKE
LIVING ITSELF AN ART,
THAT IS THE GOAL."
HENRY MILLER

94

"To walk in money through the night crowd, protected by money, lulled by money, dulled by money, the crowd itself a money, the breath money, no least single object anywhere that is not money. Money, money everywhere and still not enough! and then no money, or a little money, or less money, or more money but money always money. and if you have money, or you don't have money it is the money that counts, and money makes money, but what makes money make money?"

By Henry Miller
From: Money and How it Gets that Way

"From now on I hope always to stay alert, to educate myself as best I can. But lacking this, in future I will relaxedly turn back to my secret mind to see what it has observed when I thought I was sitting this one out. we never sit anything out. we are cups, constantly and quietly being filled. The trick is, knowing how to tip ourselves over and let the beautiful stuff out."

Ray Bradbury

PeOPLe SHAring AT A CreAtivity GAthering with SARK, June 1992

"regarDing the "DARK SiDe" and creativity: I Dont like to Think of it As THAT — I like to think of sunlight and SHADe..."

"THe Brightest sunlight produces the DARkest sHADows..."

"I WAs in A group with About 30 people, And when we started, I DiDn't think any of Them were very creative. By The middle, I HAD seen THAT They were more creative than I could HAVe ever iMAGineD!"

Q: any suggestions About sHowing My work? I'm sHy and Don't let it out Much.

A: CHoose Kind people to see it. People who will Be gentle with you and your FRAGile, new Discoveries. So often, we start From A place of scarcity or low self esteem, and CHoose A critical person to look At our work. Don't Do it!

"PlAcing an AD or answering one can change your liFe! I answered an AD to Be A crew Member sailing to FiJi — no experience necessary, But enthusiAsM! I HAD plenty of THAT. I ended up MArrying The captain, and we're sailing AgAin soon"

Q: How can I Help My CHilD keep His/Her creativity Alive?

A: By nourisHing your own creative spirit. DRAW on The walls! eAt CAKE with no HAnDs! keep The gleAm in your own eye — your cHilDren will ABsorB it like plants.

96

Live your AFFIRMATIONS

One of the wonder.full ways to be inspired is through the use of AFFIRMATIONS. It is also a powerful tool for transforming negative "self talk."

Thanks to Louise Hay, H.J. Kramer, Julie Evans, and my ever growing spiritual family for teaching and sharing AFFIRMATIONS. ♡

I created a small book called Daily Miracles, which I am reproducing here for you to remove, add your own art or photos, and use to remind you that ⌣

You are Already a Miracle

GUIDE to ASSEMBLING YOUR BOOK

Cri

YOU will BE ADDING iMAGES to 7 OF the PAGES.

CUT OUT iMAGES FROM MAGaZines, or OLD photoGRAphs, or DRAW anD paint your own.

FIND or cREAte iMAGES for These AFFiRMATioNS:

1. THere Are MiRAcles everywHere 2. relax
3. Fill your HEARt with wonDer 4. you Are not Alone 5. HAve an ADventure 6. HUG A Tree
7. relax

REMove your <u>DAily MiRAcles</u> BOOK, anD eACH pAGE with A Circle in the top left HanD corner MAy Be PUNcHED, anD yArn or string ThreADED to connect The PAGES.

O

D A I L Y

M i r A c l e s

THere Are mirAcles everywHere

o

You
Are
an
inspiration

relax

YOU ARE ENOUGH

YOU HAVE ENOUGH

YOU DO ENOUGH

Fill your HEART with wonder

O

YOU
BRING
LAUGHTER
TO SO MANY
HEARTS

You Are not Alone

H A v e an A D v e n t u r e

HuG A Tree

O

ALL
YOUR
DREAMS
ARE ALREADY
COMING
TRUE

r e l a x

THIS BOOK HAS BEEN created with love and joy @

Yes!

Transform negatives

I started out with a gigantic negative.
I'm a survivor of sibling incest.
After years of Healing and recovery,
I announced to my therapist,
   "I just figured out the positive
side to the abuse!"

   She looked stunned, and curious.
I went on.

   "During those years of abuse, I
retreated into my imagination and
just lived there. It made me intensely
creative."

It was the one gleaming star in the midst of the horror.
I wish more than anything that I had never been molested, but since it happened, I needed to try and find a way of transforming that kind of awesome negativity.
It helps me to reclaim some of what was lost.
I would also like to honor all the victims and survivors that don't find one single positive thing about their being abused!
It was just my way to transform some of that negativity. My creativity was a way for me to express myself, and open some of the doors that had slammed shut.

I AM still HEALING, and HAVE BEGUN DOING inner CHILD WORK to HELP All the WOUNDED CHILDREN inSiDe ME.

THiS is the first time I HAVE written PUBLicly ABOUt the incest, and I Know thAT it can only HELP to HEAL MYSELF, and All the SHAMED, silent voices thAT MAY BE AFrAID to SPEAK. My only GOAL is HEALING.

I Believe thAT we can vse the pain to trans.Form and Give new Form to the DEEPEST, MOST DAMAGED PArts of our selves.

One of the many books to help me tremendously is called The Courage to Heal by Ellen Bass and Laura Davis.

My boyfriend at the time wouldn't read the chapter called "For Partners" and I got angry after asking many times. One night, I just ripped the entire chapter out of the book and handed it to him.

"Here! Take it home and read it!"

A year or so later, Laura Davis wrote a book called The Courage to Heal Workbook. I stood in a bookstore, looking at it, to decide

iF I WOULD BUY it. I WAS Feeling
Weary OF All this HeAling work, and
HopeD I COULD escApe this WorkBook.
FinAlly, I AskeD GOD For A "sign" and
opened the BOOK with My eyes closeD.

The pAge and PARAGrApH I turneD to
WAS my very own story of ripping the
CHApter out of the BOOK to HAnD to My
BoyfrienD! I HAD CAlled LAurA DAViS
Just After it HAppeneD, to tell Her ABout
it, and sHe HAD USeD My story in Her
WorkBook !

I BOUGHT the WorkBook.

Autobiography in Five Short Chapters
By Portia Nelson

I

I walk down the street.
  There is a deep hole in the sidewalk.
  I fall in
  I am lost... I am helpless
      It isn't my fault.
It takes forever to find a way out.

II

I walk down the same street
  There is a deep hole in the sidewalk.
  I pretend I don't see it.
  I fall in again.
I can't believe I am in the same place.
  But it isn't my fault.
It still takes a long time to get out.

III

I walk down the same street
  There is a deep hole in the sidewalk
  I see it is there.
  I still fall in... it's a habit.
      My eyes are open
      I know where I am
  It is my fault.
  I get out immediately.

IV

I walk down the
same street.
There is a deep hole
in the sidewalk.
I walk around it.

V

I walk down another
street.

120

Write more letters!

A BOOK is like A BiG letter to
the WORLD. Letters Are MORE WAYS
to sHare our spirits.
I reMEMBer Writing to MAY SArton,
the Author, anD receiving the MOST
enDEAring anD FrienDly letter in
reply, anD HoW MUCH it WARMeD Me.

I'M AstonisHeD BY the
MAGic of letters: thin pAper trAveling
MAny or FeW miles, propelleD only

Dear SARK
WHAT A DeAr
letter you sent
to me! I reee~

SARK

By words and a tiny glued stamp.
Kiss your mailperson!

STAMP OF
Approval

I believe in keeping this ART OF
letter writing alive and thriving.
Letters are truly presents for our souls.

Here are some of my favorite excerpts
from letters I've received in response
to my FIRST BOOK, A creative companion.

"I was transported to a world where
a person could hug trees, watch snails,
and take naps whenever they wanted.
You are the first true creative spirit
I've ever known. I've always had a

GOOD iMAGinAtion, especiAlly wHen I
WAS younger, But lAtely I FeeL like I've
Become too serious. I Don't Want to Be
norMAL or orDinAry! I Just want to Be
Free to Be MyseLF.
P.S. I'm only 15, so I'm not too serious yet."

"I MADE A coMMitMent to Honor M y
creAtive spirit, But soMetiMes I HeAr
this voice thAt tells me I'm not BeinG
"responsiBle." THis is why I neeDeD to
see your inspirinG BOOK. It's sucH A
confirMAtion to Know thAt there Are
other creAtive spirits sucH As you,
LivinG their LiFe in the liGHt, AnD

I'M not Alone or crazy. THANKS so MUCH
For Giving the Free spirits of the worLD
A lovely, wonDERFUL anD spiRituALGiFt—
yourseLF."

"I curleD up in BeD to reAD your Book
As you suGGesteD, even though it WAS
noon anD MOst WOULD SAY "WHY Are you
still in BeD? (incluDing MY DAD ~ He's
46 anD Doesn't Know How to relax— MAYBE
I'll MAKe HiM reAD The BooK!"

"Do reAL puBLisHeD people reAlly
reAD their Fan MAiL?"

Oh yes, Definitely! and I will answer EACH one As long As it's possible.

"I love your BOOK. Whenever I open its PAGES, it's like BEGinning to BreAthe AGAin After HOLDING your BreAth for A long time. everything ABout the BOOK SPEAKS to Me. I love the colors, your printing And the Precious, encourAGinG, Life renewing And life reminDING WOrDS. THanks so MUCH! My journey towArD A creAtive, Joy Filled life continues... "

"Dear SARK ~ Alas, no missive, papyrus, illuminated manuscript, Book of Hours or any communication sent by a citizen of the earth, could equal that magnificent Burst of colour, exuberance and Joy, as your letter was to me."

Miriam Wornum

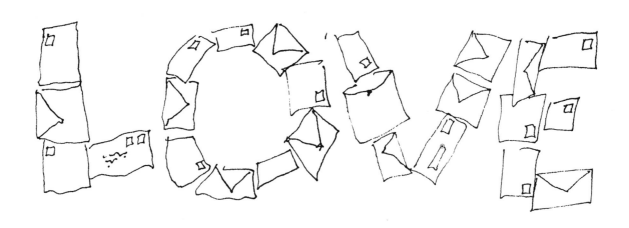

DRAW on the WALLS

I Believe we need to MAKe More Use of the WALls we live with. OFten, they're white CANVASses, JUST WAiting For us to paint theM! When I WAs creAting the cover for My First Book, I HAD A DreAM During A nAp OF HOW it WOULD look. I WOKe Up anD Drew it on the WALL with PAStel CHALK. It's still there. THe only proBlem is thAT My CAT Jupiter rUBs AGAinst it anDGeTs PAStel stripes on His BLACK Fur! Write the worD [yes] on your WALLs.

Paint rAspBerry stripes in the Kitchen!

There is A wonderful Bright plastic Paint CALLED TULIP, that comes in little Squeeze Bottles. I use it to paint my tennis shoes, and sometimes, chairs. Actually, I paint whatever needs new Life.

People have described my tennis shoes As "Melted Jelly Beans" or "psychedelic Pizza". Whenever the paint looks weary, I just ADD More. So FAr, there Are ABout A dozen layers. They're "HAppy shoes" Because they MAKE People smile.

128

ABOUT MY 250 JOBS...

My first JOB WAS AS the "WAKE UP FAIRY" in KinDerGArten. It WAS MY Best JOB. AT AGE 14, I SEWED on Buttons For people in a nursing HOME, while Also working AS A WAitress in A "BAD" PART oF town. By AGE 16, I HAD BecoME the ManaGer, DishWAsHer, WAitress anD SHort orDer Cook.

I reMEMBer A line oF very BiG Guys sitting At the counter AT 7AM, orDering eGGs. I DiDn't HAVE the slightest iDeA How to Cook eGGs, anD BAsically JuST FlAttened them on the Grill.

Then, I WOULD Deliver
the plate, and run to
the other end of The
counter.

"you, GirL! THese Aren't sunnyside up! I
ordered sunnyside up!"
I would turn and say, with my Hands
on my Hips,
"They're eggs Aren't they? eAt 'em!"
All the other Guys would roAr lAugHing,
and leAve Big tips.
    One summer, I Got A JoB putting
ruBBer tips on DARTs thAt sHoot out of
toy Guns. every few Hours, A furious
FACeD woman would APPeAr to weigh
My BAG and tell Me to work FAster.

I used to deliberately squirt glue in my eye, so I could go to the infirmary and lie down.

I saw darts in my sleep!

For years, I sold vacuum cleaners and washing machines in a department store. I was finally asked to leave when the store manager asked if I was wearing a bra, while leering at me. I asked if he was wearing a jock strap!

Then, there was the summer I taught archery at a girls camp. The only problem was, I'd never used a bow, or shot an arrow. I checked out all the books on archery in the

Library, and went there, bluffing.

The archery class was at 9 AM, with 30 whining 9 year old girls who HATED archery. By 9:30, it was already 90°, and horseflies began landing on my head, biting. Somehow, I hit a few bulls-eyes and managed to twang the string on the inside of my forearm, blackening it from wrist to elbow.

Strangely enough, it was thought that only a "real expert" would do that, and I didn't get to escape teaching archery!

When I worked as a hat check person, I used to put $10 and $20 dollar bills in my tip basket, and bet people to double my money if I could make them laugh. While they laughed, I tried finding their coats, which were unreasonably heavy and all looked identical.

Being a waitress always filled in any job gaps. Now, I always overtip in restaurants. Countless "temporary" jobs came and went, and I remember frantic hours at new switchboards in offices, disconnecting everyone.

Most of my sales jobs involved "Demonstrating" the product, and I demonstrated calculators, blenders, crepe makers, coffee machines, hair dryers, food processors, scissors, popcorn makers and photo albums... yes, photo albums!

I would stand in a store aisle, with a photo album full of fake family pictures, "your family photos could be here."

I remember wearing a 75 pound sandwich board and mask, handing out coupons. Mercifully, I don't recall what it was for. Obviously I survived all my jobs, and they all

HELPED to FORTIFY MY DETERMINATION
to DO something else... anything else!

I've Been "SELF EMPLOYED" AS A writer
AND ARtist FOR 14 years, AND it's true
THAT MY PAYCHECKS were non-existent
FOR A long time, But I continued to
create. I'm the toughest Boss I know,
AND Also the Best. One of MY Best JOB
Benefits is unlimited naps AND wearing
PAJAMAS AS work clothes.

I Believe that there's room FOR every
Person to work AT A JOB they love,
AND we need to MAGNIFY that Belief
in our society.

MAKe your work your DreAM, or
Be sure it leADs to your DreAM.
IF it Doesn't Do either oF these,
Quit sooner rather than later.

Yes,
You can!

MAKE little signs THAT SAY [Yes] AND POST THEM
ALL over your House

Yes. It is A power. Full word. Yes can affect
Us subliminally, even when we're not
Concentrating on it. Yes can move us in
FASCINATING Directions and trans.Form our
thoughts. I MADE this sign For you !

Y e s

Don't you love when they draw these little scissors?

137

Be WHo you Are anD the Money
will Follow

T Here were DAys I Ate KetcHUp
SanDwicHes. I useD to look in My
refrigerAtor anD SAy
"WHo lives Here? why Dont they Buy
FooD?"
I WAS DrAwinG, writinG, strUGGLinG,
LivinG Life. I thouGHt I HAD to pAy
For HAppiness By HAvinG no Money!
I now know thAt isn't true.
People SAy "Do wHAt you Love anD the
Money will Follow." I think it HELpS
To unDerstAnD thAt we MUst Be

HOW TO relax ABOUT MONEY

relax. Your money is not your life! it just seems that way sometimes. True wealth is inside of you. learn to cultivate money miracles. Go back to money innocence. Be who you truly are and the money will follow. You are safe. if you find yourself worrying about money, why were you lost in the first place? read "Money and How it Gets that Way" by Henry Miller. Make friends with money. Money is like love-the more you give away, the more comes back. Watch the movie "it's a wonderful life." When any money flows in for you, it's time to help others. Help them now. Money was invented to be shared. Start a revolution: refuse to believe in recessions. We need to rewrite recession to read: Money recess. remember recess? You got to go outside, kick a ball, and feel free from school. We all need to feel free about money! Take a deep breath. What you are worth is not about money. relax. You are safe

Being A Wonderfull Friend

Open your ♥ wide. let your Heart lead the WAY. Follow your insights. extend surprising invitations. read the SAME BOOKS. Serenade each other. Write a poem on the sidewalk with colored CHALK. MAKE A BOOK of your friendship memories. HAVE A private Dance recital AT A PARK. MAKE A PAPER Doll of your friend, with clothes. WASH EACH other's HAIR. Have A picnic with only Desserts. MAKE A DIORAMA in A SHOE BOX. Give small treasures found in nature. recite poetry in TanDem. Go For A Moonlight Hike. if there is anger, wait until one of you Forgets, then CALL and SAY, "Do you want to play?" SHAre feelings SAFely. Plan A Friendship ritual together. Send endearing letters. Be willing to Be separate. learn to FORGive each other. HAVE A tea PArty: WEAR HATS and EAT plenty of COOKIES. cultivate COMPASSION. Sit in the sun together and LAUGH. plan the next FIFTY years of your FriendShip. Be your own "Best" Friend. A PAIR of Friends is likely to do anything!

WHO we truly Are, to DO WHAT we love.

For many years, I HAD Known I WAS A writer and ARtist, and WASn't DoinG it, or BeinG it. InsteAD, I HAD 250 JOBS to "PAY the Bills." THe ProBleM WAS THAT My writinG and ARt GoT lost in the MiDDle OF All those JOBS.

THen, I "stARVeD" For yeArs WHile I WAS ActuAlly DoinG My ART.

THere is A MiDDle route Between these 2 extremes, and I'M still learninG ABout it.

Many people HeLPeD Me DurinG the yeArs OF KetcHuP sandwicHes, and the Author Henry Miller WAS one.

It helped me so much to read that he would go outside, throw his arms in the air and say "I owe everyone!" He also figured out a plan to have dinner at a different friend's house every night— it worked! Much of his writing supports the idea of creating despite poverty, and especially, creating-no-matter-what.

Another person to help me tremendously is named David. While I lived at the Victorian Hotel of Arts and Music, trading art for rent, he sent money for food and stamps and library fines. Most of all, he believed in me, and supported that belief with money for many years. That helped give

Me the Faith to continue creating.

My dear friend Helen was the first person to commission a piece of my art, and then pay me for it from her job as a waitress. My list of gratitude is long, and I give thanks every day.

Do your art (whatever it may be)
Find a believer/supporter (or several)
Trade and barter (especially for rent)
Pay close attention to the miracles
Follow the path of your dream
Wherever it may lead!

Give money AWAY
cʌ

THere Are many ways to Give money AWAY. Using your creativity to Help others is A FABulous way. (It is A way to Circulate Good energy.)
I created A poster to Advertise A Book sale to Benefit the library, and they raised A record Amount of money.

IF you HAVE A FrienD in transition, or worrieD About money, MAIL them some anonymously.
cʌ FinD places THAT neeD your energy anD Give some AWAY. cʌ

We think THAT money is limiteD, But it is truly unlimiteD, and can expand According to our prayers and Beliefs.

iMAGine yourseLF MAGiC

I remember riding
My Bicycle when it
could still be a Horse.
I'd PACK some Kind of
lunch and ride until
My "Horse" and I were
tired. sometimes, the
territory seemed rough
and FAR AWAY From Home, BUT THAT HeLPed ADD
to the MAGiC.
sometimes, while reading A Book sitting in the
leAFy seat of My Apple tree in the BACKyArd,
I could disAppeAr into the pAges and Become
the Pippi Longstocking that I knew lived

inside me. I can still capture that magic today, and plan to live that way always.

It helps to spend time with children because their vision of magic is so clear. A few years ago, I made treasure maps, and hid them under bricks in my garden.

Now, those maps are "mysteriously" gone, and I imagine the answer is... Magic!

Live your Adventures!

cw

At age 20, I wanted to live in Paris. While on a train in Switzerland, a man told me to go to a bookstore called Shakespeare & Co.

"Tell George that Bob referred you." I found the bookstore, across from the Notre Dame Cathedral, and the man called George was eating a whole Sara Lee cake out of the tin with his fingers. When I said that Bob had sent me, he paused for a moment, with crumbs falling to the floor.

"Well, then! Hurry upstairs to the rare library and serve tea and gingerbread! Hurry along!"

I climbed some steep and crooked stairs, and found the rare library. There was gingerbread steaming on a breadboard, and people sitting in rocking chairs, waiting to be served.

After tea, I came downstairs, and George thrust a cigar box full of French money into my hands.

"Here! This is the money box. Take care of the store for an hour or so while I go out."

I didn't speak a word of French, and had to trust people to give and take correct change.

Boit D'Argent

Argent

The "hour or so" stretched into the rest of the afternoon.

George said that I could live at the bookstore in exchange for helping with the books.

My bed was up a ladder, behind a purple velvet curtain, in a nook between the bookshelves. A poster on the wall across from my bed proclaimed

To Live Here You Must Read A Book A Day

It was a perfect place for me. Books balanced in impossibly precarious stacks. Tiny, narrow rows had been made to walk through the piles. Thick dust held the place together, and it vibrated with literary History.

I soon found out that George rarely remembered my name, or whether I had helped out or not. So sometimes, I spent my time exploring Paris...

I think I was an "adventure specialist" for a long time.

WHATever place FASCinATeD Me, I
went there. My youthFUL exuBerance
CArrieD Me in anD out oF Many
Precarious anD tantaLyzinG situAtions.

I Do recoMMenD ADventures.
    HAve As Many As possiBle.
StuFF your experiences into All
your cells anD truLy:

L i v e   y o u r   ADventures

Find inspiring people

Inspiring people Are vitamins for our spirits. They come in All kinds of Disguises and Descriptions. If you open your HEART to Being inspired, they will Appear.

One of my Favorite endlessly inspiring people was Miriam. She told me this story About being young in the 1900's and traveling Around the world with Her parents. "I would Be in

Singapore or some such place with my parents, and my sister and I would just stay in bed reading. My mother would come in and say, "Get off your filthy mattresses and see the temple of a thousand steps!"

But we wouldn't budge. Late at night, after our parents were asleep, my sister and I would sneak out, and hire a rickshaw to drive us to the red light districts and see things they never dreamed of! I would carry a scimitar in my lap ~ I had no idea how to use the thing ~ I just carried it to look threatening!"

153

Inspiring people help us to experience life in a new way.
The delight moves us.
Another inspirational woman is the poet Maya Angelou. She beams inspiration.
Her voice fills a well way inside me. When I heard her speak before an audience, she absolutely filled the auditorium with her incandescent presence.
In the darkness, you could see every heart leaping out to greet her, glowing. Her songs, words and poetry made ecstatic melodies for us to hear.

MAdeleine L'enGle, the Author, tells stories and weaves All the spirits in the room together.

Cw:

Author, speaker RAM DASS, speaks like A root Beer FLOAT: Fizzy, FAMiliAr and refreshinG.

Cw:

All oF my FrienDs inspire me too. I Believe thAT inspiration Can illuminAte tiny PArts of ourselves and Help them to Grow.
When we speAK oF A DreAM, or CreAtive iDeA, an inspirAtionAL FrienD can

HELP Give it the juice to take shape.

How can you tell if A friend is inspiring?

After spending time together, you will feel lighter, happier and bursting with some kind of new energy.

It can be quiet energy, and it may not reveal itself until later, but you will begin to recognize the feel of inspiration.

Then you can expand upon it, search it out, spend time there.

Bask in the light of inspiration. Soak up the slanted rays of its energy.

Once we begin to spend time with inspiring people, we will become more inspiring ourselves.

It will stick to us.

I wish you absolute inspiration.

it's rare

it's free

and makes us full

Most of all, inspire yourself!
Find a tree, and sit at it's roots
and listen

Pick up a rock, and hear it speak

The moon is our nightlight,
The sun our everglow...

The world will turn eagerly
towards you to hear your inspiring

Words and songs, see your paintings and drawings, touch your sculptures, drink your films and embrace all your inspiration!

Let your inspiration feed others, and give them the juice to grow, and to glow.

See you in dreams, and telepathic communication, and perhaps at a picnic for inspired souls, or in a city of angels...

Bless you,
SARK
Valentine's Day
Magic Cottage
San Francisco 1992

Write to me! Send me Something inspiring...

BY
First
Class
Miracles

PUT
STAMP
upside
DOWN

From
your
House

SARK
in care of
To CelestiAL ARTS
Mine P.O. BOX 7327
Berkeley CA
94707

From my inside child to yours

More WAYS To Be involveD...

BOOKS:

A creative companion
How to Free your creative spirit
1. 800. 841. BOOK
11.95

Inspiration sandwich
stories to inspire
our creative Freedom
1. 800. 841. BOOK
14.95

TAPE:

A creative companion
AUDio tAPE
1.800.841.BOOK 10.95

How to Be an ARTiST
FullsiZe 3.95 (23x35)
DeMi 3.50 (4¾x22)½

JUST For MoM
FullsiZe 4.95 (23x32)
DeMi 3.50 (4¾x20)

Posters:
CAll 1.800.841. BOOK
or 510 845 8414

CATALOG:

THE ReD Rose CATAloG
CAll 1. 800. 451. 5683

To order the ReD Rose CATAloG:
A WonDer. Full CATAloG!
FeATuring SARK's ART Quality
(11x14) posters, Greeting CARDS, StAtionery
A speciAL thanks to everyone AT The ReD Rose

SARK rides A creative cycle

To SubScribe to the SARK nAp club newsletter (BeGinning OCT. 92)
SenD $15 (4 issues) to CelestiAL ARTs P.O. BOX 7327 Berkeley CA 94707

To reQuest A SARK GAthering or seMinAr CAll 510.845.8414

Yes

161

MORE GOOD STUFF

The Henry Miller Library
Highway one (1/4 mile south of nepenthe)
Big Sur CA 93920
408 667-2574
open every day except monday
during summer ★
call for off
season hours ★

A fascinating collection of Henry Miller
and friends in a redwood grove ஃ
you will be welcomed here.

ஃ your public library
is full of good stuff ஃ
Go there. Help them.

The Letter exchange
A place to meet other
letter writing people
by mail. Very unusual
PO BOX 6218
ALBANY CA
94706
3 issues $18

Yes! SARK is writing another book...

THE
TRANSFORMATION
GAME
Available in stores
or call the creators
206·937·0783
PO BOX 16225 Seattle 98116
WHAT A WONDEROUS GAME!

Books ♡ love these people and I deeply thank them ♡

PHIL WOOD

DAVID HINDS

JO ANN DECK

SAL GLYNN

special thanks to: Peggy Millin
"angel editor"

There is a great tribe of dearhearts at Celestial Arts and I thank:
Marie♡ George♡ Sheri♡ Rachel♡ Nancy♡ Nicole♡ Brook♡ Torri♡ Leili♡ Maureen♡ Steve

Thanks To: • love Bubbles over • PlayHouse PARADISE Island Minneapolis White Bear Lake New York City Telegraph Hill San Francisco Martinique Cafe The Dalai Jamaica Big Sur Minnehaha creek Filbert steps •

"love's majesty"
Adrienne ♡ Ken
"the continual unfolding of love"
to my grandParents who were there in the beginning ♡

Miriam Wornum
"My Dear Friend and Mentor"

♡ Robert Brewer Hamilton young
"ancient angel"

WHAT A FABULOUS GUY!
♡ My Brother andrew
"Who tells me truths"

Nanew ♡ Marcus
"angel twins"

GOD
"Who is all·ways right in the Midst of everything (and every·one·)"

Joann ♡ Richard
"Laughter abounds"

Vimala ♡
"an extraordinary woman"

Open Heart Adventure
♡ Larry Rosenthal
"Who is right there at the center"

emily claire ♡
"Fairy godchild" and Amazon Poet

What a Woman
♡ Susan Harrow ♡
What a woman

What a cat
Jupiter
"My spirit guide"

Cecilia ♡ Lulu
"Jupiter's sister and Mom"

Goddesses "They guide us"

My Parents
"Who gave me Life"
Marje ♡ Arthur

Robin ♡ John
"a couple of adorables"

Susan Beardsley
"My Big Sister"

♡ Doug Hall and His very ♡ Merry Band of trained Brains!

"The yes Group"
♡ Cindy ♡ Lauren ♡ anne

♡ ♡ Helen Grieco
A.K.A. "Heaven"
"A True Friend"

♡ Deidre Sommers
"Storyteller in another language"

♡ Rose Frances
"Creative spirit"

David E. Early
"peep"

Gary Rosenthal
"My "Being" teacher"

♡ Henry Miller
"My Mentor"

Molly Robertson
"Healing Hands and words"

Sarah ♡ Fred ♡ Kate
"A Tribe of angels"

Kathryn ♡ Aja
"2 twinkle toes"

Mary ♡ George
"Musical sprites"

♡ Ameur Ben Arab
"what a dear heart"

Christina Merwin ♡
"Amazing Grace"

Laura B.
"celestial pixie"

♡ Debbie Lair
"Hey woman!"

Stephanie Dong
"My 9 year old teacher"
and always Gibi ♡

My "Fairy godparents"
George ♡ Diana
"Functional Family Camp"

163

WHAT IS A SARK?

SARK:
Susan
Ariel
Rainbow
Kennedy

Born
1954
Minneapolis
Minnesota

First Job:
Wake up Fairy
(Kindergarten)

First Book:
Mice From Mars
(Age 10)

Attended
Minneapolis
Art
Institute
(1960)

escaped
From
High school
(1972)

Attended
University of
Tampa, Florida
(1972-74)
Majored in travel
Adventure, Theatre

Attended
University of Minnesota
(1974-76)
Majored in
Journalism
and Wild living

Graduated!
School of
Communication
Arts
(1978)
Degree in
Radio/TV production

World
Travel
(1978-80)

rode a
Bicycle 3,000
Miles
(1979)
lots more wild living

Appeared
in
San Francisco
AKA "SARKFrancisco"
1981

resident Artist
Victorian Hotel
of Arts and Music
(1982-84)
"Ate too many
Hard Boiled eggs"

Weekly drawing
Published
San Francisco
Chronicle/Examiner
Sunday Paper
1983-1987

Created
"SARKs San Francisco"
Weekly Feature
Drawing and text
1987-1988

Created
SARK T-shirts
1986-88
Created
SARK Greeting Cards
1987-88

Discovered
A place for
SARK at
The Red Rose
Store and
Catalog
(1989-)

Created a
Dozen posters,
napshirts,
Spirit Cards,
Affirmation
Books, Greeting Cards,
Stationery
(1989—)

Wrote
A Creative
Companion
How to Free your
creative spirit
1990

Was
Discovered
By Celestial
Arts
1990

Found
the
Magic Cottage
1989
Found Jupiter
1989

Wrote
Inspiration
Sandwich
Stories to inspire
our creative
Freedom
(1991-92)

Had
250
Jobs
Ages
14-24

Plan to:
expand my
spiritual
practice or
write more
Books!

Follow
My
Heart's
Desire